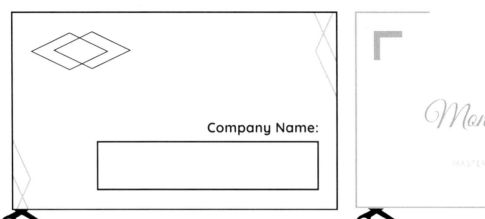

Company Name:

MW01078022

Money Magnet

MASTER OF LIFE AND LUXURY

YOUR BUSINESS CARDS

Fill in the blanks, cut them out and carry them with you.

NAME

Title

I AM _____

MANIFESTING ANYTHING I WANT

For manifesting purposes only.

Name:

DREAMER • BELIEVER • ACHIEVER

Mobile: (   )
Address:
Email:
Website:

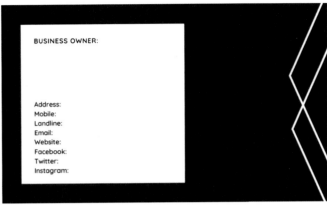

BUSINESS OWNER:

Address:
Mobile:
Landline:
Email:
Website:
Facebook:
Twitter:
Instagram:

OWNER OF AN ABUNDANCE MINDSET

Mobile:
Landline:
Office Address:
Official Email:
Official Website:
Facebook @
Twitter @
Instagram @

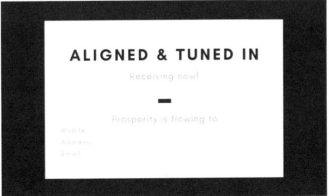

ALIGNED & TUNED IN

Receiving now!

—

Prosperity is flowing to

Mobile:
Address:
Email:

Gift Voucher

FOR THE AMOUNT OF

SEE BACK FOR TERMS & CONDITIONS

$

GIFT CERTIFICATE

JUST FOR YOU!

$

For manifesting purposes only.

$ ____

GIFT CERTIFICATE

TERMS & CONDITIONS

Present this certificate.

This certificate can be used multiple times.

Keep in a safe place.

NON-TRANSFERABLE

____ $

TERMS & CONDITIONS

This voucher is redeemable for cash.

It is non-transferable and exclusively made for you.

This voucher can be combined with other vouchers and is valid with other promos and offers.

VALID UNTIL _____

BANK OF ABUNDANCE

1111

Date | Y Y Y Y | M M | D D

Pay to the Order of _____

$ _____

_____ / 100 Dollars

🔒 **Security Features included · Details on back**

Abundance Memo _____ Per _____

‖∎ 8888 ‖∎   ∎∶ 11118 ∎∎∣ 123 ∎∶   123 ∎∎∣ 456 ∎∎∣ 8 ‖∎

- - - For manifesting purposes only. - - -

BANK OF ABUNDANCE

1112

Date | Y Y Y Y | M M | D D

Pay to the Order of _____

€ _____

_____ / 100 Euros

🔒 **Security Features included · Details on back**

Abundance Memo _____ Per _____

‖∎ 8888 ‖∎   ∎∶ 11118 ∎∎∣ 123 ∎∶   123 ∎∎∣ 456 ∎∎∣ 8 ‖∎

Manifested on: _____

Signature or Stamp

I am so happy and grateful because money is coming to me from various sources on a continuous basis.

Manifested on: _____

Signature or Stamp

I am so happy and grateful because money is coming to me from various sources on a continuous basis.

BANK OF ABUNDANCE

1113

Date | Y Y Y Y | M M | D D

Pay to the Order of _____

£ _____

_____ / 100 Pounds

Security Features included · Details on back

Abundance Memo _____ Per _____

|| ▪ 8888 ||▪ ▪: 11118 ▪|| 123 ▪: 123 ▪|| 456 ▪|| 8 ||▪

For manifesting purposes only.

BANK OF ABUNDANCE

1114

Date | Y Y Y Y | M M | D D

Pay to the Order of _____

$ _____

_____ / 100 Dollars

Security Features included · Details on back

Abundance Memo _____ Per _____

|| ▪ 8888 ||▪ ▪: 11118 ▪|| 123 ▪: 123 ▪|| 456 ▪|| 8 ||▪

Manifested on: _____

Signature or Stamp

I am so happy and grateful because money is coming to me from various sources on a continuous basis.

Manifested on: _____

Signature or Stamp

I am so happy and grateful because money is coming to me from various sources on a continuous basis.

BANK OF ABUNDANCE

1115

Date ☐☐☐☐ ☐☐ ☐☐
Y Y Y Y M M D D

Pay to the Order of _____ $ ☐☐☐☐☐☐

_____ / 100 Dollars

Security Features included - Details on back

Abundance Memo _____ Per _____

||▪ 8888 ||▪ ▪▪ 11118 ▪▪▪ 123 ▪▪ 123 ▪▪▪ 456 ▪▪▪ 8 ||▪

For manifesting purposes only.

BANK OF ABUNDANCE

1116

Date ☐☐☐☐ ☐☐ ☐☐
Y Y Y Y M M D D

Pay to the Order of _____ $ ☐☐☐☐☐☐

_____ / 100 Dollars

Security Features included - Details on back

Abundance Memo _____ Per _____

||▪ 8888 ||▪ ▪▪ 11118 ▪▪▪ 123 ▪▪ 123 ▪▪▪ 456 ▪▪▪ 8 ||▪

Manifested on: _____

Signature or Stamp

I am so happy and grateful because money is coming to me from various sources on a continuous basis.

Manifested on: _____

Signature or Stamp

I am so happy and grateful because money is coming to me from various sources on a continuous basis.

BANK OF ABUNDANCE

1117

Date   Y Y Y Y   M M   D D

Pay to the Order of _____

$ _____

_____ / 100 Dollars

Security Features included · Details on back

Abundance Memo _____ Per _____

|| 8888 || 11118 123 123 456 8 ||

For manifesting purposes only.

BANK OF ABUNDANCE

1118

Date   Y Y Y Y   M M   D D

Pay to the Order of _____

$ _____

_____ / 100 Dollars

Security Features included · Details on back

Abundance Memo _____ Per _____

|| 8888 || 11118 123 123 456 8 ||

Manifested on: _____

Signature or Stamp

I am so happy and grateful because money is coming to me from various sources on a continuous basis.

Manifested on: _____

Signature or Stamp

I am so happy and grateful because money is coming to me from various sources on a continuous basis.

BOARDING PASS
First Class

PASSENGER   DATE ☐☐☐☐☐☐   SEAT

FLIGHT   FROM   CLASS

TO   **FIRST CLASS**

GATE   BOARDING TIME

A ☐☐   ☐☐:☐☐

BOARDING PASS
First Class

PASSENGER

FROM   SEAT

TO

FLIGHT   DATE

GATE   BOARDING TIME

A ☐☐   ☐☐:☐☐

For manifesting purposes only.

BOARDING PASS
First Class

PASSENGER   DATE ☐☐☐☐☐☐   SEAT

FLIGHT   FROM   CLASS

TO   **FIRST CLASS**

GATE   BOARDING TIME

A ☐☐   ☐☐:☐☐

BOARDING PASS
First Class

PASSENGER

FROM   SEAT

TO

FLIGHT   DATE

GATE   BOARDING TIME

A ☐☐   ☐☐:☐☐

I CHOOSE WEALTH AND ABUNDANCE.
I AM WORTHY OF ALL GOOD THINGS.
I LOVE ABUNDANCE.
I INVITE WEALTH INTO MY LIFE.
WEALTH IS MY BIRTHRIGHT.
BEING PROSPEROUS IS GOOD FOR ME.
MY INCOME IS GROWING AND GROWING.
MAKING MONEY IS EASY AND EFFORTLESS.
MONEY FLOWS INTO MY LIFE.

ALL GOOD THINGS ARE COMING TO ME NOW.
I KNOW I DESERVE IT.
MY INCOME IS GROWING HIGHER AND HIGHER.
I FEEL GOOD ABOUT WEALTH AND DESERVE IT IN MY LIFE.
WEALTH IS FLOWING TO ME.
I AM GRATEFUL FOR THE COMFORT THAT MONEY PROVIDES TO ME.
I AM SURROUNDED WITH ABUNDANCE.
EVERYDAY IN EVERY WAY I AM BECOMING MORE AND MORE THE PERSON I WANT TO BE.
I SEE MYSELF AS HAPPY AND THAT IS WHO I AM.

BOARDING PASS
First Class

PASSENGER

DATE □□□□□□

SEAT

FLIGHT

FROM

CLASS

TO

FIRST CLASS

GATE
A □□

BOARDING TIME
□□ : □□

BOARDING PASS
First Class

PASSENGER

FROM

SEAT

TO

FLIGHT

DATE

GATE
A □□

BOARDING TIME
□□ : □□

For manifesting purposes only.

BOARDING PASS
First Class

PASSENGER

DATE □□□□□□

SEAT

FLIGHT

FROM

CLASS

TO

FIRST CLASS

GATE
A □□

BOARDING TIME
□□ : □□

BOARDING PASS
First Class

PASSENGER

FROM

SEAT

TO

FLIGHT

DATE

GATE
A □□

BOARDING TIME
□□ : □□

I AM PRODUCTIVE.
THERE IS NO LIMITATION TO MY SUCCESS. THE SKY IS THE LIMIT.
I CAN BE, DO AND HAVE ANYTHING I WANT.
SUCCESS AND PROSPERITY IS A CHOICE I MAKE.
MONEY IS FLOWING TO ME EASILY AND EFFORTLESSLY.
PROSPERITY IS IN EVERYTHING I DO.
OPPORTUNITIES COME MY WAY.
I AM ATTRACTING ONLY THE GOOD INTO MY LIFE.
THE LAW OF ATTRACTION IS WORKING FOR ME.

EVERYTHING I TOUCH TURNS TO GOLD.
I HAVE THE FREEDOM TO DO, BE AND HAVE ANYTHING I WANT.
MY SUCCESS AND ABUNDANCE GIVES ME JOY.
I GIVE PERMISSION TO ALL GOOD THINGS TO COME INTO MY LIFE.
SINCE I CAN HELP OTHERS WITH MY WEALTH I MAKE SURE I STAY WEALTHY.
I AM GRATEFUL FOR THE COMFORT MONEY PROVIDES TO ME.
THERE IS LIMITLESS ABUNDANCE FOR ALL AND I GET WHAT'S MINE.
I AM A MONEY MAGNET THEREFORE MONEY IS CHASING ME.

BOARDING PASS
First Class

PASSENGER

DATE ☐☐☐☐☐☐

SEAT

FLIGHT

FROM

CLASS

TO

FIRST CLASS

GATE
A ☐☐

BOARDING TIME
☐☐ : ☐☐

BOARDING PASS
First Class

PASSENGER

FROM

SEAT

TO

FLIGHT

DATE

GATE
A ☐

BOARDING TIME
☐☐ : ☐☐

For manifesting purposes only.

BOARDING PASS
First Class

PASSENGER

DATE ☐☐☐☐☐☐

SEAT

FLIGHT

FROM

CLASS

TO

FIRST CLASS

GATE
A ☐☐

BOARDING TIME
☐☐ : ☐☐

BOARDING PASS
First Class

PASSENGER

FROM

SEAT

TO

FLIGHT

DATE

GATE
A ☐☐

BOARDING TIME
☐☐ : ☐☐

MONEY FLOWS FREELY INTO MY LIFE.
I AM WORTHY OF RECEIVING NOW.
I AM WILLING TO KEEP ACCEPTING ABUNDANCE INTO MY LIFE.
I RELEASE ALL NEGATIVE BELIEFS ABOUT MONEY.
I FOLLOW MY PATH AND TRUST THE HIGHER POWER.
I AM SURROUNDED BY PROSPERITY AND ABUNDANCE.
I LIVE THE LIFE OF MY DREAMS.
I AM ATTRACTED TO MONEY AND MONEY IS ATTRACTED TO ME.
I AM WORTHY OF THE BEST THAT LIFE HAS TO OFFER.

I KEEP ACCUMULATING LARGE SUMS OF WEALTH.
I RELEASE ALL NEGATIVE THOUGHTS AROUND BUILDING A LIFE OF ABUNDANT WEALTH.
I ONLY DESERVE THE BEST OF THE BEST.
I ENJOY MY WEALTH.
I CIRCULATE MY MONEY AND IT COMES BACK MULTIPLIED.
I ONLY EXPECT THE BEST.
I DESERVE FINANCIAL ABUNDANCE.
I AM GRATEFUL FOR EVERYTHING I HAVE AND WILL HAVE.
I LOVE MONEY AND MONEY LOVES ME BACK.
I ENJOY MY NEW LIFESTYLE.

✈ BOARDING PASS
First Class

PASSENGER   DATE ☐☐☐☐☐☐   SEAT

FLIGHT   FROM   CLASS

TO   FIRST CLASS

GATE   BOARDING TIME

A ☐☐   ☐☐ : ☐☐

✈ BOARDING PASS
First Class

PASSENGER

FROM   SEAT

TO

FLIGHT   DATE

GATE   BOARDING TIME

A ☐☐   ☐☐ : ☐☐

For manifesting purposes only.

✈ BOARDING PASS
First Class

PASSENGER   DATE ☐☐☐☐☐☐   SEAT

FLIGHT   FROM   CLASS

TO   FIRST CLASS

GATE   BOARDING TIME

A ☐☐   ☐☐ : ☐☐

✈ BOARDING PASS
First Class

PASSENGER

FROM   SEAT

TO

FLIGHT   DATE

GATE   BOARDING TIME

A ☐☐   ☐☐ : ☐☐

ANYONE CAN BE WEALTHY, INCLUDING ME.
I RECEIVE FROM MULTIPLE SOURCES.
MONEY FLOWS TO ME ON A CONTINUOUS BASIS.
I HAVE AWESOME IDEAS AND THE ENERGY NECESSARY TO TURN THEM INTO REALITY.
WHEREVER I LOOK I SEE PROSPERITY IN ITS MOST BEAUTIFUL FORMS.
I AM SO GRATEFUL FOR MY LIFE.
I ASK FOR AND ALLOW ABUNDANCE INTO MY LIFE.
EVERYDAY IS THE PERFECT DAY.

MONEY IS COMING INTO MY LIFE AND SOMETIMES I DO NOT KNOW WHERE IT IS COMING FROM.
I HAVE MULTIPLE SOURCES OF INCOME.
I CHOOSE TO LIVE IN PROSPERITY.
I AM IN THE FLOW.
IF OTHERS CAN DO IT, SO CAN I.
THERE ARE NO LIMITS FOR ME.
MONEY COMES TO ME NATURALLY.
I CAN SEE CLEARLY NOW.
I AM IN A CONSTANT INFLOW OF MONEY.

MARRIAGE CERTIFICATE

NAME OF GROOM

NAME OF BRIDE

DATE OF MARRIAGE

PLACE OF MARRIAGE

Birth Certificate

NAME

DATE OF BIRTH   SEX   F ☐   M ☐

BIRTHPLACE

MOTHER'S NAME   FATHER'S NAME
MAIDEN NAME

MOTHER'S BIRTHPLACE   FATHER'S BIRTHPLACE

CERTIFICATE OF ACHIEVEMENT

THIS CERTIFICATE IS PRESENTED TO

_____

In recognition of

_____

_____   _____
Date   **Signature**

Certificate of Achievement

THIS CERTIFICATE GOES TO

_____

in recognition of

_____   _____

DATE   SIGNATURE

BANK STATEMENT

Name:
Address:
Account #:

Statement Period:
Customer Ref #:

Beginning Balance:
Deposits:
Other Credits:

Withdrawals:
Ending Balance:

DATE	DEPOSITS	AMOUNT

SUBTOTAL

BANK STATEMENT

Name:
Address:
Account #:

Statement Period:
Customer Ref #:

Beginning Balance:
Deposits:
Other Credits:

Withdrawals:
Ending Balance:

DATE	DEPOSITS	AMOUNT
	SUBTOTAL	

CERTIFICATE OF TITLE FOR A VEHICLE

TITLE NO.   VEHICLE ID NO.   DATE ISSUED

YR. MODEL   MAKE   MODEL   BODY TYPE

COLOR   PURCHASE DATE   ODOMETER   LICENCE PLATE

OTHER VEHICLE DETAILS   VEHICLE PHOTO

OWNER NAME

SIGNATURE

CERTIFICATE OF OWNERSHIP

AWARDED TO

_____

FOR _____

AWARDED THE _____ DAY OF _____ 20 ___

_____

SIGNED

VIP ENTRANCE TICKET

EVENT:

Date:

Location:

1111

VALID FOR UNLIMITED RE-ENTRIES

$

ENTRANCE AND FOOD STUB

8888

SEC   ROW   SEAT

DATE:

PLACE:

PREMIUM ACCESS FOR

TICKET NUMBER:

VALID FOR
UNLIMITED
RE-ENTRIES

ENTRANCE AND
FOOD STUB

EXCLUSIVELY FOR:

VALUE:

TERMS & CONDITIONS

Present this premium ticket.

Can be combined with other tickets, vouchers and coupons.

EXCLUSIVELY FOR:

SPECIAL TICKET

VIP Entrance

Event:

Date:

Admit One

Ticket #

Present this ticket.

EXCLUSIVELY FOR:

Special Entry Pass

EVENT DETAILS:

DATE:
TIME:
LOCATION:

Admit One

Date:

One person per ticket.

Ticket #

Admit
One

Exclusively for

TERMS AND CONDITIONS

- Tickets cannot be exchanged or transferred under any circumstances.
- Lost or damaged ticket(s) will not be entertained.
- Latecomers will only be admitted during suitable breaks.
- No ticket, no entry.

THIS TICKET ENTITLES
YOU TO ONE ENTRY

ADMIT ONE · 604760 · 604760

ADMIT ONE · 604760 · 604760

ALL ACCESS PASS

Details:

Becoming *the best version of myself*

MEMBERSHIP CARD

For

Card No.

✳ **CLARITY** ✳

GOLD CARD

8888 1111 1234 1111

GOOD THRU __ / __

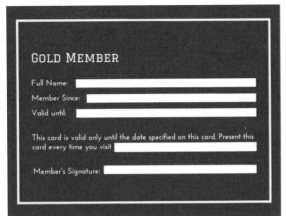

GOLD MEMBER

Full Name:

Member Since:

Valid until:

This card is valid only until the date specified on this card. Present this card every time you visit

Member's Signature:

Persistence

FOR CUSTOMER SERVICE CALL THE UNIVERSE

111

TIME TO SUCCEED

GO

NOW

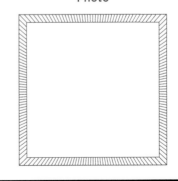

VIP
PASS

Photo

JUST START
THE REST WILL COME

 **STAY POSITIVE**

I am unstoppable

Make it happen

 **T A K E A C T I O N**

DREAM BIG

MY THOUGHTS BECOME THINGS

I am stronger than my strongest excuse

WHAT I FOCUS ON EXPANDS

I deserve it.

IF NOT NOW, WHEN?

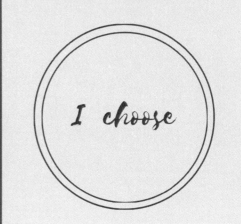

I choose

 **I AM AMAZING**

1 year
=
365 opportunities

grateful

 BELIEVE

ASK AND RECEIVE

I have a plan

Never stop receiving

GOAL GETTER

ALWAYS MOVING FORWARD

Dream Life

I do what I love

BLESSED

DESIGNING MY LIFE

Focused

THANKFUL

FEARLESS

WONDERFUL

I receive
what I
expect
to receive

TUNED IN

Faith
+
Belief
=
No Limits

Success

everything
comes
at the
perfect time

Freedom

VIBRATIONALLY
ALIGNED

COMMITMENT

BRIGHT IDEAS

Patience

DETERMINATION

inspiration

REACH FOR THE STARS

PEACE OF MIND

opportunity

Accomplish

CHECK OUT OTHER BOOKS BY
AGRIM RANGANATHAN ON AMAZON LIKE THE
MANIFESTATION JOURNALS, WHEREIN YOU'LL FIND
THE 5X55 METHOD, HABIT TRACKERS, GRATITUDE
JOURNALING AND MUCH MORE!

IF YOU HAVE QUESTIONS OR COMMENTS FEEL FREE TO EMAIL SD.INTERNATIONAL.INC@GMAIL.COM
DID YOU LIKE THIS BOOKLET? PLEASE CONSIDER LEAVING A REVIEW OR RATING ON AMAZON.

SPREAD THE WORD AND HELP AGRIM HELP OTHERS AS WELL.
THANK YOU AND HAPPY MANIFESTING! ★★★★★

BONUS!!! Download your FREE affirmation printables here:

Share your vision boards and your manifestation tools here in this Facebook group!

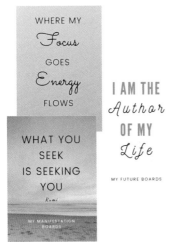

VISION BOARDS IN BOOK FORM

WOULD YOU RATHER HAVE A VISION BOARD THAT YOU CAN CARRY AROUND? YOU DON'T WANT ANYONE TO LOOK AT THE VISION BOARD ON YOUR WALL BUT RATHER KEEP IT PRIVATE? THEN THIS VISION BOARD IN BOOK FORM IS RIGHT FOR YOU!

THE PAGES ARE HALF EMPTY AND HALF RULED, SO YOU CAN PASTE PICTURES OR DRAW IN THE EMPTY AREAS AND PUT INTO WORDS WHAT YOU WANT TO ACCOMPLISH.

THERE IS ENOUGH ROOM TO ALSO ADD AFFIRMATIONS.

Made in the USA
Monee, IL
05 October 2023

43998746R00026